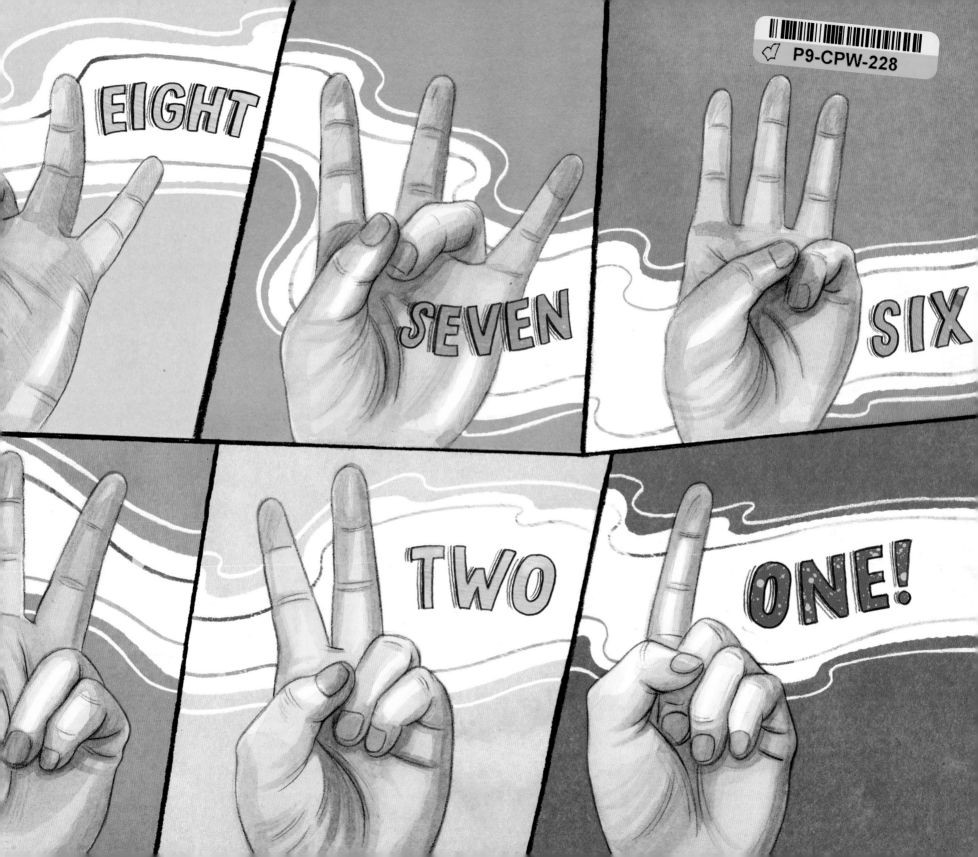

To Ann.
Thank you to Karen Greenberg, Julia Maguire, and Marietta Zacker
for their invaluable guidance.
—D.R.

For Molly, the fastest girl I know.
—E.B.

THIS IS A BORZOI BOOK PUBLISHED BY ALFRED A. KNOPF

Text copyright © 2021 by Dean Robbins
Jacket art and interior illustrations copyright © 2021 by Elizabeth Baddeley

All rights reserved. Published in the United States by Alfred A. Knopf,
an imprint of Random House Children's Books, a division of Penguin Random House LLC, New York.

Knopf, Borzoi Books, and the colophon are registered trademarks of Penguin Random House LLC.

Visit us on the Web! rhcbooks.com

Educators and librarians, for a variety of teaching tools, visit us at RHTeachersLibrarians.com

Library of Congress Cataloging-in-Publication Data is available upon request.
ISBN 978-0-593-12571-7 (trade)—ISBN 978-0-593-12572-4 (lib. bdg.)—ISBN 978-0-593-12573-1 (ebook)

The text of this book is set in Recoleta Alt.
The illustrations were created using pencil, watercolor, acrylic, and digital.
Book design by Nicole de las Heras

MANUFACTURED IN CHINA
August 2021
10 9 8 7 6 5 4 3 2 1
First Edition

THE FASTEST GIRL ON EARTH!

Meet Kitty O'Neil, Daredevil Driver!

written by
Dean Robbins

illustrated by
Elizabeth Baddeley

KITTY O'NEIL

Alfred A. Knopf 🐎 New York

She could not hear the motor rumbling.
But she could feel it in her bones.
The flat desert stretched out in front of her.
A mountain rose in the distance.

Photographers snapped pictures of her rocket-powered car.
Mechanics checked the three wheels.
Newspaper reporters scribbled in their notebooks.

Fans cheered.
She could not hear their cheering, but she could feel it in her bones.

She tapped her pedal.
The motor revved.
Vapor streamed into the air.

She gripped the steering wheel.

10, 9, 8, 7, 6 . . .

Kitty O'Neil was the speediest kid in Corpus Christi, Texas.
She loved the wind whipping through her hair.
The blur of trees and grass and clouds.
All her senses sharpened.

Kitty begged her father for a ride on their old lawn mower.
She pumped her fists.
"The fastest girl on Earth!"

Kitty lost her hearing in a childhood fever, but that didn't slow her down.
Not even a little.
She went faster and farther than everyone she knew.
Faster and farther in everything she did.

Swimming.

Diving.

Jumping.

Kitty grew up to be a daredevil.
An athlete so fearless that crowds gathered to watch her in action.

She became a stuntwoman, filming exciting scenes for movies.

Kitty set records as the fastest water skier and the fastest boat racer.

But what she wanted most was to be the fastest driver.

She chose a rocket-powered car called the Motivator and started training to break the women's land-speed record of 308 miles per hour.

Kitty could not hear a countdown, so she asked a crew member to sign the numbers with his fingers.

At zero, Kitty slammed the pedal to the floor.

Kitty practiced going faster

and faster

and faster

without losing control.

Finally, she was ready to go faster than any woman on Earth!

Kitty slammed the pedal to the floor.
The motor vibrated!
The wheels churned up dust!

The Motivator blasted across the desert!

In seconds, Kitty was going 100 . . . 200 . . . 300 miles per hour.
She struggled to keep the car from spinning out of control.

The Motivator shook.
Kitty's senses sharpened.

618 miles per hour!

Kitty eased up on the pedal.
The Motivator slowed.
The shaking stopped.
The dust settled.

Kitty pumped her fists.
She had smashed the land-speed record!
She was . . .

the fastest woman on Earth!

That day, Kitty O'Neil became a new American hero.
A toy company made a Kitty action figure.
A film company made a Kitty movie.
Everywhere she went, fans cheered.

Kitty could not hear their cheering,
but she could feel it in her bones.

AUTHOR'S NOTE

I became interested in Kitty O'Neil (1946–2018) after a member of my own family lost her hearing. Kitty lost hers as an infant due to a fever from measles, mumps, and smallpox, but she didn't let deafness get in her way. "Deaf people can do anything," she told a newspaper. "Never give up!"

Kitty was born in Corpus Christi, Texas, of Cherokee descent. She always loved exciting sports, winning swimming and diving competitions and even training for the 1964 Olympic diving team. She moved on to hang gliding, scuba diving, skydiving, and motorcycle racing. She set speed records on water skis and in boats. Her fearlessness led to work as a stuntwoman in the movie business, where she filmed thrilling jumps and car chases.

In December 1976, Kitty set out to break the women's land-speed record in the SMI Motivator, her three-wheeled, rocket-powered car. Driving on a clay flat in Oregon's Alvord Desert, she reached a top speed of 618 miles per hour. Her world record—an average of two runs—was measured at 512 miles per hour. That was more than 200 miles per hour faster than the old record!

Kitty devoted herself to helping children with disabilities, particularly those with hearing impairments. She inspired them to conquer their fears and follow their dreams, just as she always did.

"I'm not afraid of anything!" Kitty declared.

KITTY'S WORLD RECORDS

Women's land-speed record, 512.706 miles per hour • Fastest quarter-mile in auto history, 412 miles per hour • Fastest time in a funny car (a race car with large rear wheels and a one-piece fiberglass body), 365.21 miles per hour • Women's waterskiing speed record, 104.85 miles per hour • Women's water speed record, 275 miles per hour • Women's record for a free fall into an airbag, 180 feet

KITTY'S ROCKET-POWERED CAR

In 1976, Kitty O'Neil set the women's land-speed record in a supercar called the SMI Motivator. Here are some facts about this amazing vehicle.

- It was thirty-nine feet long.
- It had three wheels, like a tricycle.
- It had a pointy needle nose.
- It weighed 3,000 pounds.
- It had a tiny cockpit that Kitty, who was tiny herself, barely squeezed into.
- It used fifty pounds of fuel every second.
- Its hydrogen peroxide rocket produced 13,000 pounds of force against Kitty's 100-pound body.
- Kitty could drive it a mile in only fifteen seconds.
- The Motivator was very hard to control, but Kitty used her world-class driving skills to keep it on track.
- The car went so fast that it took Kitty five miles to bring it to a stop.

RESOURCES

Ford, Doug. *Unstoppable: The Kitty O'Neil Story.* Golden, CO: Doug Ford Engineering LLC, 2013.

Gregory, Mollie. *Stuntwomen: The Untold Hollywood Story.* Lexington, KY: University Press of Kentucky, 2015.

Ireland, Karin. *Kitty O'Neil: Daredevil Woman.* Irvington-on-Hudson, NY: Harvey House Publishers, 1980.

Phinizy, Coles. "A Rocket Ride to Glory and Gloom." *Sports Illustrated,* January 17, 1977.

Sandomir, Richard. "Kitty O'Neil, Stuntwoman and Speed Racer, Is Dead at 72." *The New York Times,* November 6, 2018.

Silent Victory: The Kitty O'Neil Story (Carson Productions and Channing/Debin/Locke Productions, CBS-TV movie starring Stockard Channing as Kitty O'Neil), 1979.

Thacher, Alida M. *Fastest Woman on Earth.* Mankato, MN: Heinemann-Raintree, 1980.

KITTY'S STUNTS

Stunt performers help create the exciting scenes you see in movies and television shows. They drive fast cars, ride on galloping horses, and make daring leaps.

Stunt performers use special equipment and follow strict rules to make their work as safe as possible. For example, they wear protective gear and jump into soft airbags. Their safety precautions don't appear on screen, so the stunts look more dangerous than they really are.

Kitty O'Neil was one of the world's greatest stunt performers. She became famous for her record-breaking jumps and her expert driving skills.

KITTY'S SPORTS

Kitty O'Neil was a top athlete in an incredible range of sports.

Boat racing • Car racing • Diving • Dune buggy racing • Hang gliding • Horseback riding • Ice skating • Jet flying • Karate • Motorcycle racing • Mountain biking • Scuba diving • Skydiving • Snowmobiling • Swimming • Trampoline jumping • Waterskiing